JUST

REMINISCE

By Jean Mitchell

Please note: Photographs used are thanks to family,

friends and of course the cats.

I do not own the rights to the other images used.

© Poetry Copywrite_JeanMItchell_Author2022

2

Farewell to Nurse Rosie

Oh, where, oh where has Rosie gone?
Wherever can she be?
She's gone away to foreign parts.
Beside the Zuyder Zee.
To work in a Renal Clinic
Where we have all heard tell,
That all the rooms are kidney-shaped
And the bed-pans are as well!
The clinic's an old haunted windmill.
So Rosie, dear Rosie, beware
Of an evil old ghost, called Wandering Hans
Appearing nightly there!
But, all out good wishes go with her,
Whether travelling by ship or Pan-Am.
For there will be an English Rose
'Midst the tulips of Amsterdam!

Ode to a Treasure

Oh Ron, I wish your work was done
Then, we could drive out in the sun
And have ourselves a little fun,
Instead of work all day!

Rooms to paper, ceilings too
Taking time, the whole day through
Makes me wonder, when will you
Take time off to play?

But, I help the best I can
By feeding up the 'inner man',
All your favourite menus plan
So you won't fade away.

Play your favourite records too,
So that you will not be blue
Thinking you've too much to do
Each and every day

Take heart Ronald, don't you know,
Only three more rooms to go
To complete your bungalow
Then put your paints away!

Then, to show how much I care
I'll let you have the best armchair
I'll run my fingers through your hair,
And soothe your cares away!

Then, after half-an-hour or so
I'll go and get your rake and hoe
The garden won't dig itself, you know!
Don't let time slip away!

ROY (LORD OF THE SQUARE DANCE)

He strides into the dance hall
With a sparkle in his eye,
His record player ready,
And the microphone held high.
Foot tapping to the music
And his old familiar stance,
With a cry of "Square-em-up!"
He leads us in the dance.

He sets our heads a-reeling,
And ladies skirts a-twirl.
It's 'Do-si-do' and 'Eight-chain-four'
He'll have you in a whirl!
He's given so much pleasure to
So many lucky folks,
With his special brand of humour
(And crafty little jokes).

The precision of his calling
Is known both far and wide,
The dancers flock to see him,
Their partners by their side.
If ever you should hear him,
By some very lucky chance,
Then tune your ears in carefully,
He'll lead you a 'merry dance!

So, come to Wessex Wheelers,
You're sure to have a ball,
With Roy Howells as your Caller,
The *GREATEST* of them all!!

Ode to Yvonne

I'm sixty today and I'm on my way
To collect my 'Old Age Pension'
My hairs turning grey, my legs giving way
Like the parts, I'd rather not mention!

I'm losing my mind and lately, I find
As soon as I get into town,
I forgot what I came for, my memory goes,
I'll have to start writing things down!

I'm having 'Hot Flushes' (I pretend they are blushes)
My breathing just comes in short pants,
But, sixty or not I'll give all that I've got
And wait till you see me 'Line Dance'!!

Bob's Wind Rising

We heard a strange sound arising,
From the toilets at Sand Bay
That noise it really was surprising
Maybe there's thunder on the way,
So don't go out tonight
Keep your tin hat on tonight
Robert Shatford's on the loo

Listen, the din is getting louder
With it there comes an awful pong
If you should need to uses those toilets
You won't wish to linger long
So don't go there tonight
Just have to hang on tight
Robert Shatford's on the loo

We called a great investigation
Measured it on the Richter Scale
In the experts estimation
Robert's caused a force ten gale!
So don't go for a stroll
When that thunder starts to roll,
Robert Shatford's on the loo

Jenny bottled all that wind-power
Sold it off to British Gas!
Now she's rolling the money
It's all due to Robert's lass
So let's all raise a glass
To the thing that came to pass
From Robert Shatford on the loo!!

Annie of Sand Bay

If you should spend a weekend in Sand Bay, down in the West,
In lovely heated chalets, with food that is the best.
Just watch out for a waitress, who stalks the camp canteen,
With spotless cap & apron, she's the fastest ever seen.
Her name is Annie – she serves the fastest breakfast in the West.

You go into the Dining Room, but before you reach your chair,
With pad and pencil ready, Annie's waiting there.
With cries of "What's yer order, cornflakes, prunes or juice, or oats?"
She'll have it on the table, while you're taking off your coat.
"Next course" she yells, "I'm ready, its' sausage, eggs or fish"
You're halfway through your breakfast and she whips away your dish.
They call her Annie, and she totes the fastest toast rack in the West.

At lunch, the same old story, before you've time to blink,
She's cleared away your pudding, and bringing you a drink.
At night, she'll serve you dinner, you'll find it much too hot,
You leave it there to cool, and find, she's pinched the blinkin' lot.
And brought along the next course, pink ice cream and some cheese,
Before you get your spoon stuck in, she cries" Coffee or some teas?"
Hooray for Annie – she serves the fastest dinner in the West.

You say "Farewell" to Sand Bay, with teardrops in your eye,
You're full of indigestion pills, and Annie's apple pie.
She's standing in the doorway, a-stacking of her plates,
And strapped upon her feet, you spy a pair of roller skates.
At last, you know the secret of her supersonic speed,
As she zooms around the tables, another crowd to feed.
We'll miss you Annie
The fastest little waitress in the West!

<u>Decorating</u>

Ron is papering the kitchen, not a pretty sight to see,
Paste and paint-pots all around him, cant get by to make the tea!
Scissors, pencils and a plumb-line, paste-brush, roller, all the gear.
Needed for the job he's doing, I don't dare to get too near.

"Watch that corner, I've just done that!" hear him shout "Just keep away!"
"Don't go leaning where I've painted, why don't you go out and play?"
Wait until he wants his dinner, then there'll be a song and dance!
He'll expect it at the right time, even though there's been no chance.

To even get close to the cooker, or even make a cup of tea!
He'll be wanting stew and dumplings – NOT until the kitchen's free!
So, get your skates on, dearest husband, finish the job and get it right
I'll be getting my best dress on, we'll go out and eat tonight!!

Dreams

If I had money, I would buy
A chalet on a mountain high.
I'd sit on the porch, in my rocking chair,
And breath in all that good fresh air.

I'd feel the warm sun on my face,
For me, there'd be no finer place.
I'd light the barbeque at five,
Feeling so great to be alive.

A steak would soon be sizzling there,
For me and Old Hound-Dog to share.
A glass or two of good red wine,
This would be my dream divine.

But alas, it's only dreams for me,
For I've only bread and cheese for tea.
My pension won't stretch to things so fine,
I'll just be content with what is mine.

A little room, a roof o'er head,
A table and a cosy bed.
Enough to keep wolves from my door,
Do I really need to wish for more?

Bugs!

I went on a visit to Georgia, my daughter and husband, to see
The house and the weather was perfect, just how you'd like it to be,
"Don't venture out in the sunshine without sunscreen your skin,
you will burn!"
"And don't forget cream for mosquitos, once bitten it's too late to
learn!"

Now, the blackflies and redflies you'll notice, the stableflies,
deerflies and fleas,
They creep up and bite, whether daytime or night, you never can be
at your ease!
There are horrible creatures called Chiggers that give you one
heck of a bite!
There are gnats, big as bees, that go for your knees
And the ticks that come out in the night!

There are bugs that are too bad to mention, they're big and they're
fat and so mean,
But the worst of the bunch, that will eat you for lunch
Are the bugs that no-one's ever seen!
These invisible beasts are least welcome, 'coz on nice bits of flesh,
they're real keen,
They go by the name of 'NO-SEE-UMS!
And they bite you, where no bugs have been!

Ballad For Charlie

Charlie has travelled far over the sea,
"England has nothing to offer" said he.
"In a far away country, a fortune I'll earn,
And when I'm a rich man, maybe I'll return"

He'll never return, he'll never return,
I know in my heart, he will <u>never</u> return!

Away he sailed, on the treacherous main,
Leaving only a daughter, to bear his name.
He sent a few letters about his new life,
Then told of three babies, and a bonny new wife!

The years passed by, and the letters were few,
Tales of no work, just a photo or two.
Fears for his safety, began to cause pain,
His young daughter feared she'd not see him again.

The days seemed so long and the nights were unkind,
And Charlie's new fortune, seemed harder to find.
Weighed down by great sadness, this wandering lad
Began to think England would not seem so bad!

Then, one sad day, came a knock at the door,
Standing outside, was a 'Man of the Law'
"I've come here to tell you your father is dead,
His tired heart snapped beating, I'm sorry" he said.

Oh Charlie! your spirit could never be tied,
Lonely, you travelled and lonely, you died.
And those who have missed you and loved you the best,
Will pray you've found peace, in your 'Haven of Rest'

'He'll never return, he'll never return,
I knew in my heart he would never return

Ruby Anniversary

Can it be all of forty years, I can't believe it's true?
It seems like only yesterday, I stood at the altar with you.
Where are all those years we shared, vanished in the air,
Yet, look at all that we've achieved, since we became a pair.

We've walked life's path together – we've had our ups and downs,
But, you'll agree, the fun we've had, far outweighs the frowns.
Two bonny daughters came along to complete our family
And what joy and happiness they brought to you and me!

You've worked so hard throughout the years, to make our future
sure,
The day seemed so much brighter, when you came in through the
door.
When times were hard, we struggled on, believing we'd get
through,
The love we shared together, we knew was always true.

I've loved you from the moment I met you at the dance.
I put my trust in your dear hands, with never a backward glance.
As we celebrate together, our Ruby Wedding Day,
I give you thanks, for loving me,
In your very special way.

Emma

What are you thinking, Emma, my love
Placidly watching the world go by?
Trapped in your wheelchair, unable to walk
Who does it bother? Not you but I.
The people who love you, want only the best,
Struggle to give you all they can give,
Willing you strength, to stand and grow tall,
Shake off your bondage, and live, Emma, Live!

"Why are doing all this?" Emma sighs,
"You are the ones who need pity, not me,
Yours is the world, full of heartaches and tears
Living in my world, I'm totally free!"
"My world is lovely, and dreamy and glad.
Just need you to love me, and know that you do,
I'm happy to sit here, secure in my chair,
It's I who should really feel sorry for you!"

Finishing Me Row

I'm crazy over knitting, as all my friends will know,
And I am quite obsessive about 'finishing me row!'
When everybody's ready, and just about to go,
Despite the cries of "Hurry Up!" I'm finishing me row!

Relaxing with my knitting, by the firelight's glow,
I'll say "I'd get some coffee, but I'm finishing me row".
The TV film is over, to bed it's time to go,
But still I say "Hang on a bit, I'm finishing me row!"

We were flying to Atlanta, the taxi's set to go,
I'm sitting in the kitchen, finishing me row!
Ron planted out some lettuce, I sat and watched them grow,
"I'll weed those plants for you" I said,
"But I must complete me row!"

My husband thinks I'm crazy, he often tells me so,
I'd get right up and thump him, but I'm finishing me row.
He says when my life's ending, and it's my time to go,
I'll shout up to Saint Peter
"I'M FINISHING ME ROW!!!"

SCRUFFY

There is an old dog down our street,
Scruffy is his name.
He puts a ball down at your feet
And begs you, play his game.

I swear he smiles at everyone
Who bends to pat his back,
With a happy nature, such as his,
Friends, he'll never lack!

His coat is rough and curly,
His eyes are hazel-brown.
His tail goes round in circles
As he bounces up and down.

He loves all of the children,
He's as friendly as can be.
I wish I had one like him
To keep me company.

You know that in a crisis,
He'd never let you down.
He'd comfort you, then cheer you up,
By acting like a clown.

I know that if he left here,
How miserable I'd be.
For, although he isn't my dog,
He means a lot to me.

Jasper

Who is this, upon my knee?
Purring and sighing contentedly,
Singing a song that is just for me,
It's Jasper, the cat and happy is she!

We liked her not, when she first came,
Running to hide when we called her name.
Spitting and snarling when visitors came
We thought her wild, and she'd never tame!

But as time went by, she seemed to know
We only wanted to love her, so –
To tempt her with food was our only chance,
She'd snatch it, without a backward glance!

Then, gradually she changed her mind,
Thought a nicer home would be hard to find,
One day, she decided I wasn't so bad,
Jumped on my lap, and made me feel glad.

Look at her now, in her vintage years!
Loves being scratched behind her ears,
Purring her loudest, to let us know –
She is OUR CAT and she loves us so!!

The Reunion

They came out of the woodwork,
The faces from the past.
Some looking as they did, back then,
And others ageing fast.

How good it was to see them all,
To talk of days gone by.
They laughed and joked together,
Remembering, with a sigh –

The Pantomimes, the shows they did,
The football matches played.
Those dances on a Saturday night,
Where many 'dates' were made!

Which led, for some, to 'Wedding Bells'
And others, broken hearts.
"What happened to old so-and-so?"
That's how the question starts.

Where were all those 'absent friends',
The knew so long ago?
"She went abroad", "They went up North",
And sadly "We don't know".

They shed so many silent tears,
For those who'd passed away.
Their memories, they hold so dear,
"We won't forget" they say.

So many hands were shaken,
Addresses written down.
Promises to "look you up"
When next they come to town.

Too soon, the party ended,
They parted, with regret.
They'll remember the night forever,
THE BEST REUNION YET!!

For Paula

My daughter has gone to far-away climes,
While I am left to recall the times
I held her nestled to my breast,
Feeling brim-ful with happiness.

Not knowing how fast the years would flow,
Each days delight at watching her grow.
Her first sweet smile, her baby talk,
The hesitant steps, as she learned to walk.

I'd braid her hair and wash her knees,
And worry over each cough and sneeze.
Too soon came schooldays and growing pains,
How often I felt her tug the reigns.

Then, away to University
Oh what an anxious time for me!
Was she happy, would she do well?
I'd long to hear that telephone bell.

Then, home for the holidays, happy hours,
Talking, shopping, the time was ours
To catch up on gossip, sort out her things,
Next it was talk of Wedding rings!

Soon, she was gone, way over the sea,
Something is missing inside of me.
But I wish her great joy, for the rest of her life,
Hope she'll be happy - being a wife.
I think, with great longing of the days back then,
Knowing I'll never have them again.
But, my love will go with her, wherever she goes,
Wishing her gladness and hoping she knows
That, whatever the future, she'll always be -
One of the best things that happened to me!!

23

First Born

There's no child like your first-born, she's such a precious thing,
There'll never be another, new feelings start to spring.
Inside a brand-new mother, that words cannot express,
Your heart is overflowing with love and tenderness.

This tiny, helpless baby, is yours to love and guide,
Thro' all of life's rough pathways, safe always by your side.
The feelings for your first-born, are only known to you,
You try hard not to spoil her, but you nearly always do!

You help her through her schooldays, and then her teenage years,
You worry if she's out late, but try to hide your fears.
You're full of pride and gladness, upon her wedding day,
But try to hide the sadness, because she's going away!

You hope she will be happy, with her husband by her side,
Her childhood life is over, you have to step aside.
But, you wish her a great future, and hope one day, she'll know
Those feelings for **her** first-born, because you love her so!!

A Culinary Cock-up

Whatever's gone wrong with me sponge cake?
I did all the recipe said.
It should be all puffed up and golden,
It looks like a pancake instead!

I read the instructions they gave me,
I weighed the ingredients right.
The pans were greased to perfection,
So why does it look such a fright?

The eggs that I used were the finest.
The sugar and flour were the best!
And REAL butter I used, not cheap margarine,
So why did the darned thing go West.

The edges were all brown and crinkly,
The top and the bottom are flat.
There's a dirty great hole in the middle,
(I wonder how I managed that?)

I made the cake for me Dad's birthday,
It was meant to be his special treat.
But, look at this object before me,
Do you think it looks good to eat?

The pigs in the farmyard might like it,
If I mix it well into their swill.
It's not fit for human consumption,
(I hope it won't make the pigs ill!)

I needed to make this cake perfect,
To prove I can cook proper food.
'Cos Dad thinks I'm hopeless at cooking,
His comments are always so rude!

But, this is the third cake I've knackered,
Despite all the things I was taught.
So I think for his birthday tomorrow,
I'll present him with one that I bought!...... (earlier).

RON'S RETIREMENT

I'm sixty-five today, the Pension's on its way,
My working days are over, I won't get any more pay!

No getting up at seven, I'll be in seventh heaven!
I'll rise when I please, and take my ease –
'Til the coffee's served at eleven.

'Tis the time of life, when me and my wife
Can do just what we like,
We'll sit and talk, or go for a walk,
Might even get a bike!

My working life was fine, I enjoyed it most of the time,
But lately its been real hard graft (must be getting past my prime!)

My eyes are not so clear, I've only got one ear,
The teeth are purest plastic, I'm cracking up I fear!

My legs are not so fast, I think my "best" is past,
There's creaks and groans in all my bones,
But still, with luck, I'll last.

So it's Hip Hooray', it's my last day and I close the factory door,
To do the things I'll have time to do, what man could ask for more!

So I'm up out of my chair, and, with good friends I'll share,
A few more "swings" and Do-si-do's"
Til I join the Celestial Square

RIGHT ON CUE!

There's a buzz of excitement in Heaven,
News has come up from Lower Ground.
That "Dapper Don" Bennett is coming
The Master of the Round!

The Square Dance has just been established,
At Roy's Celestial Squares.
They dance every night in the Throne Room
You should see those angelic pairs.

But Roy said that something is missing,
And all of the angels agreed.
They should have a Round Dance Cuer,
Dapper Don is the one that they need.

So Roy had a word with Saint Peter,
As he guarded the Pearly Gate.
"When Don arrives, please show him straight in,
Don't check his cards, he's a mate!"

The crowds in the ballroom were waiting,
To welcome this popular man.
Roy stepped out and hugged his old 'soul-mate'
Shook him warmly by the hand.

"You're just what we need here, my Dapper,
Tho' my Squares are going just fine.
I've needed you cue-ing beside me,
Now it's going to be just like old times!"

So Don stepped out onto the dance floor,
Hit by the soft candle gleam.
"Take your partners for the Paradise Waltz,
I'll teach you to dance like a dream.

The old pals were happy together,
To be back "in harness" its plain,
It only remains for us left, to say
Our loss, is Heaven's gain.

THE TRAMP

He climbed into his cardboard house,
Spread papers o'er his knees.
Then, from his grubby pocket, took
His last small piece of cheese.
No bread had he to eat it with,
No tea to wash it down.
No money left to buy a drink,
Before he settled down.

To spend another restless night.
To ponder on his life.
Once he had a steady job,
Two children and a wife.
A little home, just big enough
To house his family.
He thought that he was set for life,
But then, came tragedy!

A friend called by from out the past,
They hadn't met for years.
They laughed and joked together
As they downed a few more beers.
Then, down the road and in a pub,
For whiskey and some wine,
Another drink 'one for the road'
They'd never felt so fine!

Back to the house "please stay the night,
We've lots to talk about.
My wife will gladly make your bed,
We could not put you out"!
When morning came, the friend was gone,
And all their treasures too.
The bankbooks, silver, all their cash.
Whatever could they do?

He kissed his family goodbye,
And got into his car.
He had to find his "so-called friend"
By searching every bar.
No luck had he, the weeks went by,
As farther did he roam.
With heavy heart, he turned around –
And headed for his home.

When he got there, "THIS HOUSE IS SOLD!"
The placard met his view.
His wife and children had all gone,
Abroad, with 'YOU KNOW WHO!'
So penniless, without a home,
He wanders as a tramp.
His only home a cardboard box,
In a subway, cold and damp!!

Sarah's Speciality

Sarah made the tea today
She wondered why we stayed away
No wonder, she'd done steak and jam
And sugar pancakes, stuffed with spam!
All the dogs from miles away
Thought they'd come to tea that day
Took one look at Sarah's treat
And promptly fainted at her feet!
Poor old Sarah got the 'hump'
Threw her food out on the dump
Vowed that she would cook no more
And stormed her way out of the door!
Three weeks later, to her surprise
A crop grew up before her eyes!
Where she threw her cooking out –
A harvest had begun to sprout!
First, a ham tree growing tall
Its fruit so firm and tasty fall
A pancake plant is next to show
With spam balls dangling in a row!
People came from miles to see
Sarah's special home-grown tree
TV cameras, special feature
Starred that lucky Sarah creature!
Soon our Sarah's in the money
Life is full of milk and honey
So, retired to Sunny Spain
NEVER needs to cook again!!!

<u>The Helper</u>

Emily Claire Burton came today
She helped me clean the house all day.
She brushed the rug, and swept the floor,
She even washed the kitchen door!

We took a rest, at half past three
To drink a welcome cup of tea,
Then Emily said "let's do more work
This is no time to sit and shirk!"

So off we went – a-dusting there
Polishing each and every chair,
Until I shouted "That's enough,
Poor old grandma's out of puff!"

Emily said "that's what you think!
You forgot the kitchen sink,
Then the windows must be done...
Goodness, aren't we having fun!"

But I sink into my chair,
Watching Emily, scrubbing there,
A sudden thought comes to my brain,
I think I'll let her come again! (Tomorrow!)

Clara and Daisy

There was a cow called Clara,
Who gave the finest milk,
Her tall was long and swishy
And her ears were soft as silk.

She had a friend, named Daisy
Whose coat was black and white.
Her nose was pink and shiny,
Her eyes were clear and bright.

These cows were very friendly,
And 'mooed' as you passed by.
They grazed upon the green grass
Beneath the summer sky.

Each morning, very early
The farmer came along
Carrying a bucket
And whistling a merry song.

"Good morning, my fair ladies,
How do you do?" he said
"Could you stop your grazing,
And come into the shed?"

"It's time I did some milking,
Let's make a start" said he
"So let's have lots of creamy milk
Fill up my bucket for me"

So both cows gave their best milk
To Farmer Brown, that day
His pail was over-flowing
As he went on his way

He sent the milk to Sarah
To share with Emily
They made it into custard
And had it for their tea – with Rhubarb!

Ronald's Wall

T'was on a dark and stormy night,
The thunder roared and caused a fright,
The wind was wild, the lightning flashed–
And, to the ground the back fence crashed!

Next morning, standing on the lawn,
Our Ronald saw his fence had gone.
He decided, at our great expense,
He'd have to buy a brand new fence.

But on his way to work that day,
He spied some bricks they'd thrown away.
A great idea formed in his head,
He'd try and build a wall instead.

So, a trench he dug and the concrete set,
Working every minute that he could get.
And soon, before my very eyes –
A magnificent wall began to rise.

Row upon row of bricks he laid,
(Such hidden talent he displayed)
Resplendent in his shorts and vest-
Never stopping to take a rest.

Until at last the job was done,
I thought, 'Now we'll have time for fun'
But, "No," said Ronald, "I've been hoping
To finish off the top with coping."

So off went he to the DIY
Where he found the prices much too high.
"I won't be beat," I hear him muttering,
"I'll mould the coping in plastic guttering.

So, seventeen top bricks he made,
All neatly in a row displayed.

"Now can we play?" I sweetly ask.
Thinking he had completed the task.
"Finished it?" Of course, I ain't,
It's got to have a coat of paint."
So, off he went a-painting there,
The neighbours gathered round to stare.

At the edifice, so grand and clean,
THE FINEST WALL they'd ever seen.
Let's raise our glasses, one and all,
And drink a toast to Ronald's wall.

For though his work's not always quick.
He sure knows how to lay a brick.

Tony – My Friend

He was my friend
Though he was just a little lad
A friendly smile for all – he had
It warmed my heart and made me glad
To be his friend

His legs could never walk or run
And yet, he was so full of fun
He'd laugh and joke with everyone.
My Special Friend

But, when he lost his precious sight
His courage kept his spirit bright
He tried to learn, with all his might
My little friend

He was my friend
But now he rests in final sleep,
And friends, remembering, softly weep
My treasured memories I will keep
Of my 'Special Friend.'

Bryony's Lament

When I was a tiny baby, my mummy said there'd be
A child minder called Aunty Jean, who'd take good care of me.
So Tuesday, Wednesday, Thursday I went to Aunty Jean,
Who cooked me lovely dinners and kept me sweet and clean.

We played nice games together and went for walks each day,
I thought I was in heaven, 'til that Ryan came to stay!
He pinches all my stickle bricks and steals my dollies' pram
He sings and shouts and runs about 'til I don't know where I am!

I tried hard to ignore him and played in my own way.
Oh. How I wished that Aunty Jean would send that boy away!
Aunty Jean said "NOW THEN!! Stop all this tearing about!
Sit down and make some jigsaws, then I will take you out"

I lined up all my dollies and made them cups of tea,
Along came 'Rip-roaring Ryan' and tipped it over me!
I thought I'd stand up to him, I'd show him I could be...
Just as strong as he is (but he's twice as big as me!

Aunty Jean was sensible, she sat down on the floor
And said "we'll play together and you two fight no more!
There are so many play toys, enough for two to share,
Bryony can play with these and Ryan's are over there"

But I liked his toys better than the ones she'd given me...
I offered Ryan one of mine, to swap for his best three!
We shared a double buggy, when we go out each day,
We're singing songs and Nursery Rhymes, as we go on our way

We have a swing together, go whizzing down the slide,
Then, back into the buggy, for another little ride
Back to Jeans we travel, for biscuits and some juice
The buggy makes an awful noise (the wheels are getting loose!)

Ryan sits beside me and shares my little tray,
He smiles at me, and sings a song, he's quite nice (in a way!)
We have our lunch together, we each have our own chair,
I'd feel a little lonely, if he wasn't sitting there.

I've really grown to like him, and i think he quite likes me!
Perhaps I'll ask my mummy to invite him round for tea.
But something sad is happening, my Ryan's leaving me!
His mum's having a baby, to keep him company!

But, if I ask Jean nicely, maybe she will see...
If she can get another boy, to come and play with me.
I really will miss Ryan, but, never thought I'd say...
How happy every day has been, since Ryan came to play!

The Zoo

Emily went to the Zoo today, one whole pound she had to pay
She saw the lions and the tigers too, and a bear that looked liked Winnie the Pooh.
She rode on an elephant, high and wide, with its keeper walking by its side.
There were pandas, with their eyes so big.
A camel and a pot-bellied pig.

A bright coloured parrot said "How do you do?
I've been waiting all day, for you.
I heard you were coming to see me today,
Come and give me a kiss, please don't run away"

Emily looked at his beak and then shook her head,
"I don't think I feel much like kissing" she said,
"It's time I was going, there's so much to see,
And mummy will soon take me home for my tea!"

Then she watched, as the dolphins put on a show,
Leaping up high, then diving down low.
The seals clapped their flippers and stood on their tails
Begging for fish, from big silver pails.

Emily's mummy said "We'll have to go
We have to get home for our dinner, you know,
Wave to the animals tell them "goodbye"
(Don't let them see you've a tear in your eye!"

MARRY A RON

You can't go wrong, if you marry a Ron,

He'll make you happy, your whole life long.

He'll work like a slave from morning to night,

Making you money with all of his might.

He'll love you and keep you safe from all harms,

Love you forever and praise all your charms.

Build you a home that is fit for a queen,

Make you a garden, the best ever seen!

Help you to wash up the dishes each night,

Give you a kiss as you turn out the light.

Wake you each morning, with love in his eyes

So, if you can catch one, you'll have such a prize!

He'll always be ready to be leaned upon,

So you can't go wrong,

IF YOU MARRY A RON!

Under The Greenwood

Thought that I', just for 'a gas'
Join an evening guitar class.
Bought myself an instrument,
Paid the cash, and off I went.
Started with cords A and C
Graduated onto D.
Found I could not get the sound
(Had my guitar wrong way round!)

Soon I learned both F and E
Then I mastered B and G
In three weeks, with fingers sore,
I could strum, 'Plaisir d' Amour!
So I practise every day,
Hour after hour, I play.
Eyes are crossing, fingers tire,
I must crack, 'Mull of Kintyre'.

Now I'm on the Ragtime scene,
Boy! I'm getting really keen.
Before my head can hit that pillow,
I must play that 'Weeping Willow'.
Robin tells me "Don't you fret –
You'll be on the TV yet!
Promise you, before we're through,
You'll be playing 'Song Sung Blue!"

Soon the course will have to stop,
No time left to learn some Pop,
Cheer up Robin, never fear,
I'll be coming back next year!
And its all because of Robin, I can strum a little, pick a little,
play a little song,
Yes its all because of Robin, I'll be thanking him my whole life long!

Oh, What A Life

Oh, what a life I've had,
It hasn't been all bad.
I've got no cash, just my 'old man'
He's quite a bonny lad.

We've had our ups and downs,
With lots of smiles and frown.
We rub along, just him and me,
The kids have both left town.

Our home is pretty small,
It barely held us all.
But now its size is just enough
Except when visitors call.

He's very good you see,
As long as he gets his tea.
His grubs the first thing on his mind,
I think the last, is ME!

OUT TO LUNCH

I'm going out to lunch today,
I hope it's fit to eat!
Cos I eat nothing but the best,
It had better be a treat!

At home I feast on choicest things
Like caviar and steak,
Asparagus tips and passion fruit,
And rich Madeira cake.

The finest wines, my tables grace
Best coffee and liqueurs.
My culinary skills are far
Superior to hers!

I'll bet she gives us frozen meat,
From some old supermart.
Instant spuds and stringy beans,
And MICROWAVED jam tart!

And, if she does, you bet your life,
I'll make it very plain.
If she can't do a better job.
I WON'T GO THERE AGAIN!!

Emily Claire's Song

A baby came today, to steal our hearts away.
A little girl, we thought never could be,
We waited for so long, now life is just a song,
'cos she's brought such joy to our family!

Emily Claire, Emily Claire,
My pride and joy forever, she's going to be
Emily Claire, baby so rare,
She's the greatest thing that ever happened to me!

We hoped for many years, and shed a million tears,
When we thought we'd never have a child to share!
Then suddenly, we knew, our dreams had all come true,
The babe, we had longed for, soon would be there

Emily Claire, Emily Claire,
My pride and joy forever, she's going to be
Emily Claire, baby so rare,
She's the greatest thing that ever happened to me!

Now, as we watch her play, grow stronger every day,
We thank our lucky stars, she came to be,
We'll thank her, through the years, for the laughter, joy and tears,
And the love she's giving to her Daddy and Me!

Iraq

"It just isn't fair" sighed Emily Claire,
"My daddy has gone to Iraq.
I'm feeling so sad, and my mum will get mad
If they don't tell her when he'll be back.

"I'll be ever so good, for I know that I should,
To help mummy get through each day.
I'll stay clean and dry, and try not to cry,
Though it's lonely with Daddy away!

It's three months or more, since he walked out the door
To help those poor helpless Kurds,
Who aimlessly roam, without any home.
They are just too hopeless for words!

So we must take heart, although we're apart
And write lots of letters to Dad
To tell him we care and we're proud that he's there,
And pretend we're not feeling too bad!

But, what's this I hear,
Someone's coming near
And opening my bedroom door.
It's MY DADDY I see,
And he's smiling at me.
Now we can be happy once more!!

Ant-hology

I bought me a big bag of compost,
In order to pot up some plants,
But, when I was ready to do it,
Found the compost was riddled with ANTS!!

And, as I surveyed them with horror,
I said to myself "This won't do"
"I can't use the stuff, as intended.
I'll have to ring up B and Q"

The lady said "What's the problem?"
When I told of the ants, said "good grief"
"We'll have to do something about them,
The blighters will eat every leaf!!"

"Just you check the name on the label
And tell me the type you have brought,
We'll give you a new bag of compost
Without even a second thought!"

So, into the greenhouse, I hurried,
To read what the label had said,
GREAT MILLS MULTI-PURPOSE
(NOT B and Q!!)
(Have you ever wished you were dead!

Happiness

I am happy, when a friend drops by.
When I look up at a cloudless sky.
When my sponge cake rises way up high,
And I bake a perfect apple pie!

If I hear a robin start to sing.
Or I see a eagle on the wing.
A snowdrop, heralding the spring
Hear the laughter, that a joke can bring.

I don't need to be a millionaire,
If I have a friend, my life to share!
Somebody who will really care,
Who is happy, to be always there!

Ode to Gordon Day and Oswald

Life begins at forty,
(Or so the poets say)
So, have some fun on Friday,
Enjoy your 'Special Day!'
Don't bother with the 'Phyllosan'
Or other patent brew.
Just use your own 'get up and go'
It's really up to you.
No need to take the Valium,
Throw all your pills away
Do everything you want to do,
And you'll be a GREAT DAY!

Oswald

Said Oswald, the bored little Owl,
"I think my life's terribly foul,
So, a monk I will be...
In a monastery,
"I'll look awfully sweet, in a cowl!"

Golden Day

It's 50 years since Edna took Roy

To be her special 'pride and joy'.

Vowed to love him the rest of her life,

And make him proud of his brand new wife!

The years flew by filled with laughter and fun,

Then they were blessed with a baby son.

With his auburn hair and smile so sweet,

His birth just made their lives complete.

Now, fifty years they've been together,

Through snow and sun and stormy weather.

The best love story ever told,

May their lives be always PAVED WITH GOLD.

MITCHELL'S DAILY RAG

www.dorsetnews.co.uk   **Dorset's Favourite Newspaper**   since 1932

PLEA TO THE EDITOR

That I decided to 'have a go'
At your competition, designed to find –
The person with poetic mind.
To write on "Rugby" was the theme.
The prize of a fiver, my ultimate dream.

So, brains a'wracked, my rhyme I penned,
And to your paper I did send
My little verse, about the game.
And with a flourish, signed my name!

The following week t'was in the 'RAG',
"Look, I'm in print" I proudly brag.
But, alas, since then, although I've bought
Every edition, the news I sought.
To see who won it, was my aim,
But <u>never</u> saw the winning name.

So PLEASE Mr Editor, hear my plea
And let me know, if it was me.

Reply:

I write to thank you, for my prize
The 'fiver' was a nice surprise.
(Although it was a little late!)
To be your winner, sure felt great!
Your poem really made my day
And quite made up for the delay.
So, as I finally rest my pen,
I'd like to thank you, once again.

MR MOBEY AND THE MORNING CREW

Dear Mr Mobey, I'm writing to say,
How much I enjoyed your programme each day.
While visiting my daughter, for six weeks vacation,
I tuned in each day to your Radio Station.
To hear the best music and join in the fun,
With you and your buddies on Kicks 101 (.5)
My home is in England, but on our radio
We <u>never</u> get "Country" – and we love it so.
Atlanta is gorgeous, it captured our heart,
I was full of regrets when I had to depart.
But I have great memories (and tapes of your show)
To lift up my spirits, when I'm feeling low.
So thanks, Mr Mobey, for all you have done,
To make our vacation a true "Country" one.
Keep up the good music and maybe someday,
We'll meet face to face, if you're passing my way!

YEAH BABY!!

A few months later

PPS. To send you this letter, I did my best
But sadly, I sent it wrongly addressed.
They tried to deliver it, only to fail,
And I had it returned from U.S. Mail.
So I'm trying to reach you, just once more
To say, once again, how much I adore
Your programme each morning on Kicks 101 (.5)
Here's a big "YEAH BABY" from FAN NO. 1

When Winnie Sang 'Alice Blue Gown'

A sweet little lady has just passed away,
A few days before her hundredth birthday,
Her eyes had grown dim, and her hearing had gone,
But like a 'real trouper' she still soldiered on,
And brought so much pleasure with her favourite song,
When Winnie sang "ALICE BLUE GOWN"

A tiny old lady, with figure so neat,
So full of laughter, it was such a treat.
To hear her at parties, she'd bring the house down
As all of the kinsfolk, gathered around
To hear Winnie sing "ALICE BLUE GOWN"

Her hair was a halo, whiter than snow,
And friends and family, all loved her so.
Always a smile, a pleasure to know.
But what a sad moment, when they laid her down,
And the organ played, "ALICE BLUE GOWN"

Now, she is there, at home in the sky,
Telling her family, "no need to cry"
"We'll meet again in the sweet By & By",
She's safe up in heaven, where she's found renown,
Singing her "ALICE BLUE GOWN!"

Computers Do Bite

I got me a nice computer,
To print up the words that I write.
I read all the books that came with it,
But I can't seem to get the thing right!

I type out a poem so neatly,
Save it and give it a name.
I then ask the printer to print it
But it thinks it's some kind of game!

In place of the poem I ask for,
This THING gets it into its head,
To make me feel very angry
By printing another instead!

This cannot go on much longer,
My patience is wearing thin.
If it won't do the things that I ask it,
It's going STRAIGHT IN THE BIN!!

P.S.
But I know a man who can help me,
I'll call in a "Fred's.com
He'll fix it real quick,
'Cos he's one clever dick
He'll install me a new CD Rom!

So if your computer is dying
And you think you'll call it a day.
Get Fred to inspect it
He'll soon resurrect it
And get it to work right away!

THE LEAVING

Oh Tony is leaving,
We all will be grieving
To know that we'll see him no more.
The girls will be sighing,
And moaning and crying
Their history class is no more!

No more will they read
About Venerable Bede
Or Rufus, or Harold or James
But they'll smile through their grief
For they'll feel such relief
From trying to remember such names!

Oh lets not be sad
And try to be glad
That Birminghams' gained such a prize!
So, drink up your beer
And wish him "good cheer"
And smile, as we wave our "Goodbyes!"

Tina

There is a Line Dance teacher, the best you'd ever meet.
With rhythm in her body, and magic in her feet.
She's cute and she is perky, she's always full of fun,
And when it comes to teaching, she is second to none!
Her name is
TINA
She calls the fastest LINE DANCE in the West!

If you attend her classes and you have two left feet,
It won't take long for Tina, to make you dance real neat.
She'll show you how to shuffle, and make a quarter turn,
A rolling vine, a step-side-close, you won't take long to learn.
With our friend
TINA

Who calls the greatest LINE DANCE in the West!

Quite soon she'll have you strutting, you'll even do a vine,
All you really need to do, is make sure you're in line.
There's pigeon-toes and twinkles, a hitch and kick-ball change,
If you dance with Tina, you'll go through all the range –
Of steps with
TINA

The smartest LINE DANCE caller in the West!

So pull your western boots on and come and "strut your stuff"
For once you learn to Line Dance, you'll never get enough!
Just come along to our club, you'll soon see what I mean
And learn to dance with Tina, our lovely LINE DANCE QUEEN
We love you
TINA

You're the cutest LINE DANCE teacher in the West!

ODE TO
EDNA

Oh, Edna is leaving and everyone's grieving
To think she really will go.
She's been there for years, it will all end in tears
They are going to miss her so!

How can they go on, with dear Edna gone?
And no-one could take her place.
There's so much to be done, and they'll never find one
To match her smiling face.

The work piles up high, they're wondering why
Not once did they hear Edna moan.
When it came to the crunch, she would even miss lunch
To sort someone out on the phone!

But the years fly so fast, the time's here at last
For Edna to put up her feet.
To spend time with Roy, her 'Valentine Boy'
At their cosy St Andrews Retreat.

They'll spend time together, whatever the weather
Sharing all they'll now have time to do.
So "Good Luck" we will send to our 'Wellbeloved' friend
And a HAPPY RETIREMENT TO YOU!!

Our Sarah-Jane is FORTY today
Oh, what a wonderful year.
A party is planned, and won't it be grand
With her friends and family here!

When she was a child, she was so meek and mild
She wouldn't say "Boo" to a goose.
But as she grew older, she became a lot bolder
When a teenager out on the loose!

Her Grammar School days, just passed in a haze
Of Maths, French, English and such,
But acting the fool 'stead of 'keeping the rule'
Showed she didn't rate school very much!

Said "Farewell" to her friends – joined up in the WRENS
Spent most of her time 'all at sea'.
Met Marine Martyn Burton, Sarah then felt quite certain
His wife, she just had to be.

The years rolled on by, with them wondering why
A baby just wouldn't appear!
But, after ten years, and buckets of tears
Their much-longed for daughter was here!

So, let's raise our glass, to this wonderful lass
And give her a big rousing cheer.
We'll all drink a toast, to the girl with "the most"
For GOOD LUCK IN HER FORTIETH YEAR!

40 YEARS OLD

Oh, my name is Jill and it gives me a thrill
To see you all gathered today.
I think it's' just great and we'll all celebrate
My 40th birthday.

I ought to be glad, but it makes me so mad
To see one more wrinkle appear.
There's lumps on my hips and lines on my lips
I'm just getting older, I fear.

There's a terrible crack, when I straighten my back
My eyesight is getting quite weak.
I think I can hear, if you're speaking real clear
But my knees make a hell of a creak!

But I mustn't complain, though it's perfectly plain,
I'm reaching the top of that hill.
I'm well past my prime and there'll soon come a time
To think about making my will.

But, today I feel fine, I can still 'Toe the Line'
I'll dance just as long as I'm fit.
I'm 40 so what! It isn't a lot,
Quite frankly, I don't   give a "<u>whit</u>"!!

Ode To An Oldie

Oh no, my dear Ron, you're having us on

You can't be as old as you say.

You've still got some hair, and your wit is still there,

Tho' your memory is fading away!

Your eyes are still clear,

You can just about hear, if your deaf-aid is set on high.

Your knees are quite knobbly, your tum's getting wobbly

And you put your teeth out to dry.

But watching you dance, as you sway and you prance,

I've never seen footwork so nifty.

Tho you're SEVENTY today

I just have to say

You don't look a day over FIFTY!!

Martyn's Do

There's a 'bit of a do' in the mess today
We're all invited to go.
To bid farewell to our mutual friend
To Colour Sergeant Joe!
'Twas in the year of '75
At the age of sweet sixteen,
Young Joe decided to have a go
At being a Royal Marine!
He signed on as a galley slave
A chef he learned to be.
Amid the gleaming pots and pans
A happy lad was he!

He grew to be a super cook,
He travelled far and wide.
To Ireland and to Kurdistan
With his ladle by his side.
Through sleet and snow
Where cold winds blow
In Norway's icy blizzard.

He'd sling the hash, made sausage and mash
To fill each starving gizzard!
At roasting spuds, and straining greens
Our Joe was Number ONE.
Then came the day, he heard them say
You're a Colour Sergeant, Son!
But now, it's time to say "Goodbye"

And one thing is quite certain
We'll miss him so, when he has to go
"Good Luck" to MARTYN BURTON!
But as we gather to say "Farewell"
We think he's gone quite barmy.
After all these years as a Royal Marine,
He's going to join 'THE ARMY'!

Annie Is Sleeping

Annie is sleeping, we'll just let her lie
Deep in her thoughts, of days gone by
When she was a girl and then a young bride,
With the man she had chosen, by her side.

Annie's remembering two tiny girls,
She's washing their faces and brushing their curls,
Watching them playing outside in the sun,
Laughing and giggling, having such fun.

Annie is thinking of two smiling brides,
Two handsome gentlemen by their sides.
Wishing them well as they start their new lives,
Taking on new roles, as husbands and wives.

Annie is smiling, as memories flow,
Three grandsons, a granddaughter, oh how they grow.
It was "Nan" that they ran to, when they were in tears,
For the comfort and love she gave, all through the years.

Annie is dreaming of days, long ago
Of threading her needle and learning to sew.
From covers to curtains, she used all her skills
For shortening dresses and gathering frills.

Annie thinks back to her party in May.
When folks came to wish her a "Happy Birthday"
The people all gathered from far and near.
To toast a grand lady, in her ninetieth year!

Annie is sleeping, her last earthly rest,
Happily knowing she's given her best.
To all who have known her, throughout her long life,
A good neighbour, sweet mother and wonderful wife.

Pam's Predicament

Pam said to Pete "Just take a sniff
At my uniform blouse, it don't arf wiff!
The sun is shining up in the sky,
I'll wash that blouse, it'll soon be dry"
So into the suds and out on the line,
Went the Littlewood's blouse, looking so fine.
But, whilst planting peas, Pam failed to see
That a gale-force wind coming off of the sea
Had made her blouse do a merry dance,
It leapt off the line, and headed for France!
Pam asked everyone in the neighbourhood
Thinking her blouse had gone for good.
No-one had seen it, up in the sky,
Pam thought she'd kissed her blouse "Goodbye".
The Police were alerted, they sent out the Force.
A huge helicopter flew over the gorse.
It scoured the woods, the valley, the ground
But Pamela's clothing could not be found.
Then, came a message to say they had heard
From someone who'd spotted a beautiful bird.
They rushed out to see this amazing sight,
A wonderful creature in colours so bright
Soaring high about the house,
Dipping and diving wearing a blouse!!
Made up of colours of many a hue,
Red, white, beige and navy blue.
"That's mine" cried Pam in great despair
As the bird went flying through the air.
"You thieving varmint, what a cheek!
If I catch you, I'll wring your beak!"
But the bird just flapped its' wings with glee
"Don't I look great in this?" said he.
"I think I really am 'the goods'
Just give my regards to Littlewoods!"

Heartbreak

In the still of the night, when the whole world sleeps
A mother, for her daughter weeps.
Her heart is breaking, deep in the night.
To hear that a marriage, that seemed so right
Has broken in pieces, and may never mend.
She sobs in her pillow, "Please don't let it end"!

It started with high hopes, she remembers the day,
The man claimed her daughter, and took her away
To start a new life, in a faraway land.
He promised to love her, as he took her hand.

He said "She's my angel, I'll guard her for life
I'm so proud to take her, for my dearest wife"
He was so sincere, his words we believed,
We were sure that he loved her, she'd not be deceived.

Her father is slumbering by his wife's side,
His sadness is hidden, deep down inside,
He mourns for the man he had called his 'son'
He thought he was the perfect one.

To take care of his daughter and make her his wife,
And form with her, a bond for life.
His disappointment he'll never show
His heartache, only his wife will know!

He's not one for talking, he'd rather not say
How he misses his daughter, so far away.
It's not easy to say the right things, on a phone
And so sad to know she is all on her own!

How can we help her, when we're far apart,
To hold her close, as he's breaking her heart?
Till you have a daughter, you never could tell
How, when her hearts aching, your heart aches as well!

So, all we can do, while she's feeling so sad,
Is send her the love, she knows she's always had
And, hope that with time, the healing will start,
Then, maybe, she'll find a new love in her heart

Azteca Dave

The AZTECA GRILL is a great place to eat
Where, each Wednesday evening, old friends always meet
And, ready to serve you, with food that you crave,
Is a handsome young waiter, called AZTECA DAVE
He'll serve nachos, tortillas, and soup of black beans
Great enchiladas, and hot turnip greens
Burritos and salads, shrimp in disguise
His hot Jalapenos bring tears to your eyes!

Now, AZTECA DAVE really turned on the charm,
When I showed his the cast, on my poor broken arm,
He knelt by my side, put a kiss on my cheek
Saying "Please let me bring you my 'Dish of the Week"
"Talapia fish, grilled in the finest red vino
Smothered all over in hot Jalapeno"
"Oh no, I can't take it – just grill me the fish
With plain mashed potato – that's all that I wish."

"My tummy can't take all those peppers and dips
To be honest, I'm happy with burger and chips!"
Poor AZTECA DAVE, his eyes opened wide
Said "If that's what you want, there's McDonalds outside!"
I tried hard to eat his MEXICAN treats,
But found it was out of the question
I just couldn't take his BURRITO STEAK
It didn't suit my weak digestion!

Each Wednesday evening DAVE tried hard to please
But all I could long for, was cauliflower cheese!
Now home in England, my thoughts often stray
To that wonderful MEXICAN VENUE
And that good looking waiter named AZTECA DAVE
Who allowed me to 'mess-up' his menu!

Farewell to Friends

Now is the hour
When we must say 'Adieu'
We wish you health and happiness
May good luck go with you!

Fresh challenges to tackle
(We know that you will cope.
And lots of time to get to know
Your newest grandchild 'HOPE'.

We'll miss our 'coffee mornings'
But time will soon take wing.
So all the best to everyone.
We'll see you – in the Spring!

Angus – 80 Years Old

His feet are made for dancing
There's a twinkle in his eye.
He has a cheerful greeting
For people passing by.

He's always warm and friendly
When he shakes you by the hand
He's loved by all who join him
In his Line and Square Dance band

Soon, he will be Eighty!
(Though you would never guess,
We wish him all the very best
Of health and happiness.

We'd like to be there with him
To share his SPECIAL DAY,
But we live here in England
It's much too far away!

Enjoy your birthday, Angus,
With all who love you so,
DON'T hang your dancing boots up yet,
YOU'VE MANY YEARS TO GO!!

The Sweater

Dear Sir, here is your sweater,
I regret it took so long.
You would have had it sooner
But I made the neckband wrong.

I had a mental picture of
You, standing at the wicket.
Got my stitches all mixed up
And then, had to unpick it.

Eventually, I finished it,
With hope in every stitch.
That it will keep the wind out,
When you're battling on the pitch.

A-scoring of a century
With strokes through "square" or "cover"
bowling maidens over ......"
wishes – Paula's Muvver!

Printed in Great Britain
by Amazon

33236716R00046